HOW DO YOU KNOW?

Wisdom in the Bible

ISBN 978-1-949628-12-8
Printed in the United States of America.
10 9 8 7 6 5 4 3 2 1   22 21 20 19

Published by The Pastoral Center, http://pastoral.center.

Developed in partnership with MennoMedia and Brethren Press. Series editors: Fumiaki Tosu, Ann Naffziger, and Paul Canavese. *How Do You Know?* Writer, Christopher Bowman. Project editor, Lani Wright. Staff editors, Susan E. Janzen, Julie Garber, and James Deaton. Updated design, Paul Stocksdale.

All rights reserved. Purchase of this book includes a license to reproduce this resource for use in a single parish, school, or other similar organization. You are allowed to share and make unlimited copies only for use within the organization that licensed it. If you serve more than one organization, each should purchase its own license. You may not post this document to any web site without explicit permission to do so. Outside of these conditions, no part of this book may be reproduced in any form or by any means, electronic or mechanical, including photocopying, recording, taping, or via any retrieval system, without the written permission of The Pastoral Center, 1212 Versailles Ave., Alameda, CA 94501. Thank you for cooperating with our honor system regarding our licenses.

For questions or to order additional copies or licenses, please call 1-844-727-8672 or visit http://pastoral.center.

Portions of this work © 2019 by The Pastoral Center / PastoralCenter.com. Adapted and published with permission from Generation Why Bible Studies. © 1996, 2014 Brethren Press, Elgin, IL 60120 and MennoMedia, Harrisonburg, VA 22803, U.S.A. All rights reserved.

Unless otherwise noted, the Scripture passages contained herein are from the *New Revised Standard Version of the Bible*, copyright © 1989 by the National Council of the Churches of Christ in the United States of America. Used by permission. All rights reserved.

Bible-based Explorations of Issues Facing Youth

» OVERVIEW

When conversing online, the acronym IRL stands for "in real life." The virtual world of social media, text chats, blogs, and more have the power to remove us from the real world. What we experience online can skew our perspective on what it means to be human. It can numb us, incite us, distract us, depress us, confuse us, and make us rude or impatient. Strangely, this supposedly "social" and "connected" technology can profoundly disconnect us from others.

Religious faith can also place us in a bubble, especially when it distances us from others. When we keep the prophetic message at a safe distance, obscured in theological language and abstractions, we are missing the whole point. And when we see our parish as an insider club that serves itself, we can forget the radically inclusive message entrusted to us: God's love is for *everyone*, and God expects us to transform the *whole world* through that love.

Through the incarnation, God showed up in the real world to show us that our faith is not just about talking the talk, but also walking the walk. It can be risky. It can be confusing. It can hurt. But living out our faith can also bring us great purpose, peace, and joy.

This series connects the Bible with the tough questions that youth (and adults) encounter in their neighborhood, in school, among friends, and even online. This process will help you as a leader break open these issues in a fun and meaningful way, sparking conversation and the kind of life change Jesus invites us to embrace.

» THE ROLE OF PARENTS

As children enter middle school and high school, they become more independent, self-reliant, and, well, self-centered. This can bring parents to make assumptions that this is the time to step back, giving their child more space to form their identity. While there is truth to that at some level (adolescents definitely shouldn't be smothered), this is a stage of life when parents should in fact *lean in*. The apparent confidence and bluster youth show on the outside can mask the insecurity and confusion on the inside. Youth need their parents to be involved more than ever.

» WHOLE FAMILY FORMATION

Parents are the primary teachers of their own children, and parishes are waking up to the fact that faith formation programs need to bring parents into the process if they hope to see faith passed on to the next generation. Recent studies give us more and more evidence that the role of parents is the most important factor in determining whether a child will embrace faith as they move toward adulthood. Research from the Center for the Applied Research on the Apostolate shows that parents who talk about their faith and show through their actions that their faith is important to them are more likely to have children who remain Catholic.

More about Whole Family Formation

To learn more about how your parish can take a comprehensive whole family approach to faith formation, visit **GrowingUpCatholic.com**.

While whole family events with elementary-aged children are on the rise, the role of parents can be an afterthought in youth ministry. We have designed the sessions in this series to work with or without parents present, and we encourage you to offer them as parent-child events.

If you choose to involve parents, it is important to consider before each session how to best do so. Many of the activities in this series are high-energy, creative, or silly. Some parents may need some encouragement to get out of their heads and have fun with the group. A few activities involving physical contact would be inappropriate for parents and youth to participate together, and we have noted them as such.

There are a number of ways to approach discussions with parent participation. Unless you have a small group, you will likely want to break into smaller groups for conversation. Some youth may be self-conscious and unable to be completely honest and open in a group situation with a parent present. For this reason, you may choose in some cases to assign parents to different groups from their own children, or to have separate parent and child groups altogether. Be sure to cover expectations around confidentiality. It is inappropriate for a parent (or youth) to share with another parent what their child said in a small group.

Note that even if parents and their children do not share all conversations together in the session, they will still have a valuable shared experience and can have extended conversations about it later.

❯❯ THANK YOU

The role you play in gathering, animating, praying with, and forming youth is a valuable one. Thank you for all you do to serve the church and its families!

Bible-based Explorations of Issues Facing Youth

HOW DO YOU KNOW?
Wisdom in the Bible

>> INTRODUCTION

Wisdom literature doesn't get the attention it deserves. Jeremiah lists the "counsel of the wise," along with the law of the priest and the word from the prophets as three classes of spiritual leadership in Israel (Jer. 18:18). Yet for most believers, little time is spent learning to appreciate this form of biblical instruction.

While the other styles of authorship in our Bible emphasize spectacular or supernatural stories about God's activity, wisdom literature is more down-to-earth. Waiting for a lightning bolt revelation from God, we often overlook the simple patterns of life and common-sense learning. The bumper-sticker approach to theology, wisdom literature encourages people to "get smart," to avoid trouble, and to find peace.

In its simplest form, wisdom is one person telling another how to stay out of trouble, how to find deeper meaning in life, and how to avoid a "negative" journey (walking the wrong path).

But advice needs anchors. What is sound advice in one situation is exactly the wrong advice in a different situation. Looking at contradictory advice from biblical and popular proverbs, we come to realize that truth survives the contradictions. The community of faith, together interpreting truth in each situation, guides us through difficult times.

Wisdom is also a good pathfinder. There are underlying routes of righteousness in life. Learning these routes leads to good living. Ignoring the truth of these routes leads to destruction. Certainly there may still be suffering, but a life that follows the path of wisdom will find a way through even the most difficult situations. The very heart of early wisdom is: "Be good and you will get good things in return."

But a direct challenge to that heart of early wisdom is the story of Job, a righteous man who suffered unjustly. Unjust suffering is a frequent complaint of adolescents. What is discovered in Job's story, however, is that it is from within our suffering that God becomes more clearly understood. If this is true, then in dealing with people who are suffering, wisdom would have us do more looking and listening than problem-solving and preaching.

Finally, the book of Ecclesiastes is an attempt to answer the question, "If bad people sometimes get good things and good people sometimes suffer, what should be our guide in living?" Here is a question asked by most young people in their search for meaning in life. We come to understand from Ecclesiastes that life is meant to be lived in the moment. While

> **Following the path of wisdom leads to good living, even when it winds through fields of suffering. Life is meant to be lived in the moment. While looking for the celebration, sorrow, and presence of God in each moment, we come alive to and internalize the route of righteousness.**

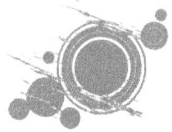

EXTENDER SESSION

Extender sessions suggest special activities related to the issue of the unit. They help accommodate the diversity of parish schedules. Since each unit is undated, participants may study units in their entirety and still participate in special events of the parish that get scheduled simultaneously with youth group time. Extender sessions can be used anytime, but the one for this unit best follows **Session 4**. Calculate now whether or not you will be using the extender session.

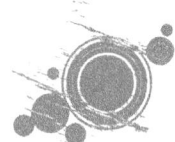

looking for the celebration, sorrow, and presence of God in each moment, we come alive to and internalize the route of righteousness.

PREPARATION ALERT

Throughout this unit, group members will be creating a list of Youth Proverbs. This list, begun in the first session and added to along the way, will be a central exercise. Learning to write one's own proverbs is a key step in learning to appreciate the proverbs written by another. Keep on hand newsprint, markers, and masking tape for the whole unit.

For **Session 3**, collect some sets of rules (*Robert's Rules of Order*, driving instructions, student handbook from school, etc.). Also select nine magazines of the same shape for use in the opening game.

For **Session 4**, prepare four people to be actors/readers in a role-play.

For additional background reading on wisdom:
- William Anderson, *Wisdom Books: Job, Psalms, Proverbs, Ecclesiastes, Song of Songs, Wisdom, Sirach (Ben Sira)* (Liguori Catholic Bible Studies series, Liguori Publications).
- Christopher Bowman, *Wisdom* (Covenant Bible Studies series, Brethren Press).
- Walter Brueggemann, *In Man We Trust: The Neglected Side of Biblical Faith*.
- Derek Kidner, *The Wisdom of Proverbs, Job and Ecclesiastes: An Introduction to Wisdom Literature*.
- Kathleen M. O'Connor, *The Wisdom Literature* (Liturgical Press).
- Susan Sink, *The Art of the Saint John's Bible: A Reader's Guide to Wisdom Books and Prophets* (Liturgical Press).

THE TEACHING PLAN: The parts of the session guide

Faith story. The session is rooted in this Bible passage.

Faith focus. The story of the passage in a nutshell.

Session goal. The entire session is built around this goal. What changes—in knowledge, attitude, and/or action—do you desire in your group?

Materials needed and advance preparation. This is what you will need if the session is to go smoothly. You'll feel more at ease if you've taken care of these details before you meet your group.

FROM LIFE TO BIBLE TO LIFE

The teaching plan we use is called *life-centered*. However, when we write each session, we always begin with scripture. We ask, what does this particular passage say, especially to youth? Each session moves from life to Bible to life. So the Bible is really at the center of this way of teaching.

In every session we try to hit upon a tough question that youth might ask. Find out what questions on this issue are important for your group. Feel free to bring your own input and invite your group members to add their own experiences.

TEACHING THE SESSION

The five step-by-step movements will carry you from *life to the Bible and back to life*. Each session takes about 45 to 50 minutes. If there is a handout sheet for the session, take note of any complementary activities and stories.

1. **Focus.** Intended to create a friendly climate within the group and to *draw attention* to the issue.

2. **Connect.** Invites participants to *express* their own life experience about the issue, through talking, drawing, role playing, and other activities. Also uses memory, reason, or imagination to get the group thinking about *why* they view the issue the way they do.

3. **Explore the Bible.** What does the Bible *say* about the issue? With a minimum of lecturing, dig into the faith story and search for answers to questions raised in the first activities. The Insights from Scripture section will help clarify the faith story. Help participants discover how the faith community understands the Bible passage.

4. **Apply** the faith story. What does the Bible passage *mean* for contemporary life? This is the "aha!" moment when participants realize the faith story has wisdom for *their* lives.

5. **Respond.** Why does the Bible passage *matter*? What will the group do about the issue in light of what they have learned from their own experiences set alongside the faith story? How can we *live* the faith story rather than pass it off as a mere intellectual exercise?

LOOK AHEAD

Here are reminders for what you need to do for the next session or two.

INSIGHTS FROM SCRIPTURE

Here is a resource for Explore the Bible. Don't try to use all the material given. Take what you need to lead the session and answer questions your group may have. Let the Insights section inspire you to think and study more about the passage for the session.

HANDOUT SHEETS

Occasionally, there will be a handout sheet to complement your session. If you choose to use this, you will need to make enough copies for the group. These sheets may include questions, stories, agree/disagree exercises, charts, pictures, and other materials to stimulate your group to think and discuss.

Generally, no participant preparation is required unless the session plan calls for you to contact selected group members for specific tasks.

>>> **SESSION 1**

WHAT IS WISDOM? >>>

>>> **KEY VERSE**

For in vain is the net baited while the bird is looking on. (Prov. 1:17)
Paraphrase: It's no use setting duck decoys while the ducks are watching.

>>> **FAITH STORY**

Proverbs 1:1-33

>>> **FAITH FOCUS**

Wisdom literature holds a special place in the Bible. This is not the stuff of preachers, scholars, or genealogists; here is material written for (and by) teachers. These people were charged with teaching the young people of the faith how to avoid the "snare" of evil and the decoys of foolishness and, in so doing, come to a good life.

>>> **SESSION GOAL**

Since youth face a constant deluge of contradictory advice, guide them to use and create "scriptural sound-bites" called proverbs to help them learn from mistakes.

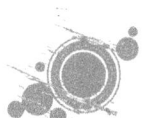

TEACHING PLAN

1. FOCUS 10 minutes

People make really stupid mistakes. If we're not too proud, it can even be funny to remember the stupid mistakes we've made. As a group, make a list of "Stupid People Mistakes" you have made over the last year or that you have seen others make. Write these *on the left half* of a large piece of newsprint taped to the wall, or on the chalkboard. Be sure to list a mistake or two of your own.

After everyone has told their "stupid mistake" stories, have the group vote on whether or not the story deserves "Top Five Stupid People Mistakes" status. Number the top vote-getters.

>>> **Materials needed and advance preparation**

- Newsprint/markers or chalkboard/chalk
- Masking tape
- Copies of the handout sheets for Session 1
- Bibles (Note: Eugene Peterson's paraphrase, *The Message*, includes a modern-language version of the Psalms and Proverbs.)
- Writing paper and pencils/pens
- Index cards
- As you prepare to teach about wisdom literature, read through the entire book of Proverbs.

> "See, I am sending you out like sheep into the midst of wolves; so be wise as serpents and innocent as doves."
>
> Matthew 10:16

>> **Option:** If you have plenty of time, make the Top Five list into a Top Ten list.

Examples:

3. The time I locked my keys in the car.
4. When I went to pick up my date I saw that she was dressed up and I was dressed casually.
1. Watching cheerleaders coming out to the field, I rode my mountain-bike into the back of a parked van.
2. A friend of mine was playing trombone with the band. He was at the top of the bleachers and lost his grip on the slide and it flew all the way down to the basketball court.

(**Note:** Abbreviate long stories to short but memorable snippets such as "slip-sliding trombonist.")

2. CONNECT 5-6 minutes

Ask: *How do we react to this list? Do we find our mistakes humorous? Do they make us angry? Are we embarrassed? Do we find other people's mistakes funnier than our own mistakes? What made the best* (Top Five) *different from the rest?* (Were they the most stupid, embarrassing, or easiest to spot?) *Do we often feel we must hide our mistakes?*

The one good thing about our mistakes is that we can learn from them. Better yet, we can help other people learn from our mistakes. Best of all, we can learn from other people's mistakes. As the saying goes, "Everyone learns from mistakes; if you're smart, you'll learn from other people's mistakes." For example, when someone walks up on stage with their fly open, everyone else in the room checks their zippers. When someone tells a really stupid joke, the rest of us think more carefully about the joke we were about to tell. **Mistakes teach us to change.**

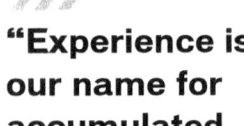

> "Experience is our name for accumulated errors."
>
> Jewish proverb

Distribute copies of the first handout sheet and read the poem, "Autobiography in Five Short Chapters." Talk about the universality of the ideas expressed in the poem. People everywhere make mistakes. Sometimes we make the same mistake several times. Eventually, however, we learn from our mistakes in order to avoid the problems of the past.

3. EXPLORE THE BIBLE 15 minutes

Shift to this activity by saying: *In the Bible, lessons about the mistakes people make are called proverbs. Thousands of years ago, these lessons were written down to help other people avoid making stupid mistakes and getting their lives all screwed up.*

Give the group a little background:

> *The book of Proverbs starts out by saying that these are the proverbs of Solomon, the wisest person in the Bible. Some of the sayings may actually come from King Solomon. Others are from the sages (wise teachers) from other times and other places.*
>
> *In collecting these sayings, the writers of Proverbs intended that everyone might get a bit smarter. The young, the simple, and even the wise can learn from the mistakes of others and all of us become foolish when we refuse to learn.*

Remind the group that the book of Proverbs is in the middle of the Bible, right after Psalms. Have everyone look at the first chapter of the book, and make the following comments:

> *Wisdom was a feminine voice in Hebrew scriptures. She calls to people in the town square and wants them to stop being such idiots. In verse 22 she asks us how long we're going to*

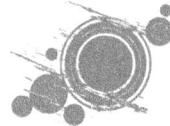

like being stupid. At its very core, wisdom literature suggests that Wisdom herself really wants us to gain an understanding of how the world works. Wisdom gives us pointers that are true for all of human history and points out that God wants us to get smart before we kill ourselves.

Then choose one of the options below.

>> **Option A:** Break into three groups, have each group draw their assignment **(Proverbs 1:7-9; Proverbs 1:10-16; Proverbs 1:17-19)** from a hat or another selection method. Distribute newsprint and markers, along with the second handout sheet, and follow instructions there. Introduce each section of Proverbs by reading the comments on the handout sheet.

>> **Option B:** Have three people read the sections of Proverbs on the second handout sheet aloud while others follow along in their Bibles. As a group, talk about each section prior to moving to the next. Ask: *What is this section saying to us? What kind of mistakes might have prompted the teachers to write down these sayings?* Close each discussion by sharing the comments. As a group, translate each key verse and write "Today's Youth Version" on a piece of newsprint.

4. APPLY 5-10 minutes

Explain that a proverb is an epigram (short poem dealing with a single thought: "A stitch in time saves nine") or a maxim (fundamental principle, truth, or rule of conduct: "Look before you leap").

By collecting and preserving proverbs, the Bible suggests that God intends that we use our brains as well as our Bibles—our smarts as well as our faith.

God's not just concerned about whether or not we get to heaven; God also wants to help us keep from making fools of ourselves and from slipping into ugly ways of living. One of the ways we get smart is to learn from our mistakes.

>> **Option A:** Give each person an index card. Then tell them to think about where they are now in their lives (their job-place, significant relationship, school situations). Ask: *Can you think of a trap you fell into which you now wish you could have avoided? Write this trap (or the mistake you made) on your card.*

Say something like:

With this trap in mind, write a proverb that would be a quick lesson for someone else entering your world. What short piece of advice would you pass along to someone you care about? Is there something you wish someone had told you about school, a first date, looking for a job, or a relationship? Try to make your saying short enough to fit on a bumper-sticker, but don't worry if it's a little longer.

When finished, share the "proverbs" with the whole group.

>> **Option B:** Look back at the list of "Top Five Stupid People Mistakes" (from Focus), and have the group name the "lesson of life" we might learn from them. On the *right side* of the newsprint or chalkboard, write the "Top Five Lessons of Life." Make the lessons as short as possible; keep them to bumper-sticker length. Number the lessons to match up with the list of mistakes. Examples (from "stupid people mistakes" listed above in Focus section):

1. Watch for grilles not for girls.
2. Don't forget, when pursing your lips—The looser the hold, the more a slide slips.
3. Look before you lock.
4. Don't assume when you groom.

"**An educated person knows many things, but one with much experience knows what he is talking about.**"

Ecclesiasticus 34:9

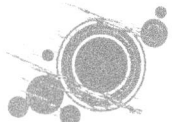

"**The man who understands his foolishnesses is wise.**"

Jewish proverb

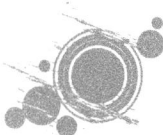

>>>
LOOK AHEAD

While God's truth is timeless and trustworthy, the sages of wisdom literature realized that different situations require different (and often contradictory) advice. Next time, we'll look at the problem of contradictory proverbs and how believers look for the path of the Lord amid the contradictions of life. One can be going the right way even though the road sometimes doubles back in the opposite direction.

Keep the "Life is Tough Enough…" poster from Session 1 for use in the next session. Recopy if necessary, and make enough room in the collection of youth proverbs to add more next time. Read Proverbs 10–22 in preparation for the next session. Copy a list of contradictory proverbs as instructed in Focus.

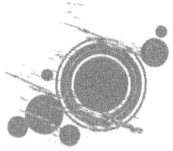

>>>
"For learning, the ear is more useful than the eye."

Jonah Gerondi

5. RESPOND 10 minutes

Everyone makes mistakes—it's part of living. The important thing is that we learn from our mistakes. The next important thing is that we are willing to share our mistakes and our learning with other people so they don't have to make the mistakes themselves.

To begin the process of helping others learn from your mistakes, create a "Life Is Tough Enough…So Get Smart!" poster which gathers up youth proverbs and displays them. These would include the index cards of Apply, *Option A,* or the two newsprint/chalkboard lists of *Option B*. On the left half of the poster write "Life is Tough Enough…" and put up the list of "Stupid Mistakes." On the right half write "…So Get Smart!" and there place the collection of youth proverbs. Keep this poster up throughout your study.
At the beginning of each session, add a biblical proverb as a memorization verse.

Close with a prayer:

*Thank you, God,
       for giving us brains and for helping us learn not to make fools of ourselves for anyone but you. Protect each of us as we go into the world.
       Help us learn what it means to live for you even when we catch ourselves making mistakes.
Amen.*

 INSIGHTS FROM SCRIPTURE

Although King Solomon's name figures prominently in the book (1:1; 10:1; 25:1), he was undoubtedly not the author of all the proverbs. (Most obvious is 31:1-9.) It is probably more important to realize that the authors were attributing their wisdom lists to the wisest person in the world.

> "God gave Solomon very great wisdom, discernment, and breadth of understanding as vast as the sand on the seashore, so that Solomon's wisdom surpassed the wisdom of all the people of the east, and all the wisdom of Egypt. He was wiser than anyone else, wiser than Ethan the Ezrahite, and Heman, Calcol, and Darda, children of Hahol" (1 Kings 4:29-31a).

This desire to attribute Proverbs to the wisest man in the world shows just how seriously these sages (teachers) took their jobs. The teachers were responsible for making their students aware and wise. Getting smart was the way to keep people out of trouble. While other parts of the Bible talk about how God gets involved in our lives and protects us from evil, wisdom literature takes a different point of view.

When Bible scholars talk about wisdom literature, they are referring to a type of biblical content that emphasizes that people can figure out right and wrong without God having to step in and zap them with a lightning bolt. "God's goodness and plan for living are evident in the world around us," say the teachers of old. "All we've got to do is learn to look and listen. Those who have ears should hear, for heaven's sake." While revelation comes at God's choosing, wisdom is available to everyone at all times. This is a good corrective to our arrogant belief that God personally handles all the little details of our lives.

In the novel *Cold Sassy Tree*, Will almost gets run over by a train. He asks, "Grandpa, you think I'm alive tonight cause it was God's will?" "Naw, you livin' cause you had the good sense to fall down 'twixt them tracks." "Maybe God give me the idea." "You can believe thet, son, if'n you think it was God's idea for you to be up on thet there trestle in the first place. What God gave you was a brain. Hit's his will for you to use it—p'tickler when a train's comin'." (Olive Ann Burns, *Cold Sassy Tree*)

In wisdom literature we have the confession that we work at faith with our brains and not just with our hearts.

Books that show this particular understanding of the world are Proverbs, Job, Ecclesiastes, some psalms, Sirach (Ecclesiasticus) and the Wisdom of Solomon. Some Bible scholars add Song of Songs, Ruth, Tobit, parts of Deuteronomy, Esther, and Amos. Even the story of Joseph (Genesis 37–50, but omitting chapters 38 and 49) is considered wisdom because Joseph gets out of trouble by using his head, not by waiting around for the sea to get dried up or the famine to be miraculously washed away. The sayings and some of the teachings of Jesus (like those in the Sermon on the Mount) show wisdom influence, as do the Gospel of John and the letter of James. In all these, people are called on to make right decisions based upon what they observe, rather than upon divine revelation. In fact, if you find a Bible story where God doesn't loudly say or visibly do a whole lot and where people are seen to be responsible for their own behavior, there's a good chance that its roots are in wisdom.

> **Some biblical books like Ecclesiasticus and the Wisdom of Solomon are considered authoritative in the Roman Catholic and Orthodox Churches, but not among our Protestant brothers and sisters. Some Protestant Bibles will include these books under the heading "Apocrypha."**

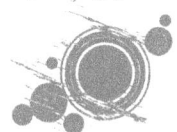

Autobiography in Five Short Chapters

by Portia Nelson, 20th-century American writer

In Real Life
Exploring tough questions facing youth today

Chapter 1

I walk down the street.
There is a deep hole in the sidewalk.
I fall in.
I am lost…I am helpless.
It isn't my fault.
It takes forever to find a way out.

Chapter 2

I walk down the same street.
There is a deep hole in the sidewalk.
I pretend I don't see it.
I fall in again.
I can't believe I am in the same place, but it isn't my fault.
It still takes a long time to get out.

Chapter 3

I walk down the same street.
There is a deep hole in the sidewalk.
I see it is there.
I still fall in…it's a habit.
My eyes are open.
I know where I am.
It is my fault.
I get out immediately.

Chapter 4

I walk down the same street.
There is a deep hole in the sidewalk.
I walk around it.

Chapter 5

I walk down another street.

Permission is granted to photocopy this handout for use with this session.

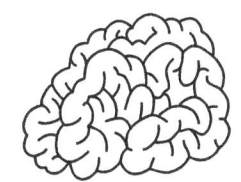

What is wisdom?

Exploring tough questions facing youth today

Proverbs 1:7-9
People who use their brains—people who don't make many stupid mistakes—are a whole lot more fun to be related to than people who mess up all the time. Proverbs 1:9 even points out that listening to your parents makes you look quite good to them and to others. But the **key verse** in this section is **verse 7**.

Proverbs 1:10-16
This section shows that people who use their brains are less likely to be sucked into the wrong group of people. How often have you heard the words, "Oh, let's just put our money together and pay for it," only to have the friends end up with the things you paid for (1:14)? And isn't it true that it gets easier to be nasty to other people when you're in a group of people being nasty? The **key verse** is **verse 10**.

Proverbs 1:17-19
People who use their brains are smart enough to realize that nasty people have their nastiness backfire on them. What goes around comes around. The **key verse** is **verse 17**.

Instructions:

1. Read your assigned section of Proverbs 1.
2. Talk together about what it means.
3. Translate the key verse into your own words.
4. Write your translation—"Today's Youth Version"—on the newsprint and tape it to the wall.
5. Explain to the larger group what that verse means to you.

Permission is granted to photocopy this handout for use with this session.

SESSION 2

IS IT TRUE OR ISN'T IT? >>>

>> KEY VERSE

Commit your work to the Lord, and your plans will be established. (Prov. 16:3)
Paraphrase: Choose to work for God and future choices will be plain as day.

>> FAITH STORY

Proverbs 10-22

>> FAITH FOCUS

Proverbs that were written three or four thousand years ago are still relevant today. Some seem contradictory, yet if we watch carefully, we find that something can be "true forever" while not being "true for always." Being true for all time is not the same as being true for all times. The proverbs of old are not righteous in and of themselves, but they help us recognize the right path in a confusing world.

It is tough to live in a world without ironclad answers. The Bible suggests that listening within a situation is just as important as collecting up answers ahead of time. Proverbs teach some specific answers, but also teach about a world in which answers are to be learned along the way.

>> SESSION GOAL

To youth awash in a sea of moral ambiguity, toss the lifeboat of biblical wisdom, which points out trustworthy ways of recognizing God even when surroundings seem confusing or contradictory.

>> Materials needed and advance preparation

- Add to proverbs poster from last session; see instructions in Focus.
- Newsprint and markers (three colors)
- Masking tape
- Paper and pencils/pens
- Bibles

TEACHING PLAN

1. FOCUS **10 minutes:** 1 minute to describe the rules, 7 minutes each problem,
5 minutes for wrap-up questions

Ahead of time: If necessary, copy last week's "Youth Proverbs" to newsprint or posterboard and edit for clarity. Using a different color marker, make a second list of popular (modern) sayings, making special effort to collect sayings that contradict each other.

Some suggestions:

Many hands make light work.
...Too many cooks spoil the broth.
He who hesitates is lost.
...Look before you leap.
A bird in the hand is worth two in the bush.
...There are other fish in the sea
Just Do It!
...Just Say No!
(Leave room at the bottom to add others.)

With yet another color, make a third list. Find proverbs from chapters 10–22 with which you might argue given different situations, or which seem to contradict each other. (Again, leave room for additions.) You might want to put them in your own words so they are easier to understand. These might include:

I. 10:10: *"Whoever winks the eye causes trouble, but the one who rebukes boldly makes peace."*
Coupled with...
13:3: *"Those who guard their mouths preserve their lives; those who open wide their lips come to ruin."*

II. 17:23: *"The wicked accept a concealed bribe to pervert the ways of justice."*
Coupled with...
18:16: *"A gift opens doors; it gives access to the great."*

III. 20:30: *"Blows that wound cleanse away evil; beatings make clean the innermost parts."*
Coupled with ...Abusive situations.

IV. 21:5: *"The plans of the diligent lead surely to abundance, but everyone who is hasty comes only to want."*
Coupled with ...Instant lottery winners.

As you begin the session, have the group vote on the following ethical dilemmas (or create your own). Count votes by having participants move to one side of the room if they agree with the statement, and to the opposite side of the room if they disagree. While no one is permitted to stand in the middle they might position themselves closer or farther from each side to indicate "strong agreement" or "slight agreement." After each vote, ask why they voted the way they did.

QUESTIONS:
Problem #1
1. If Mr. Smith cuts off Mrs. Jones' arm on purpose, Mr. Smith should be severely punished (e.g., have his own arm cut off, put in prison, etc.).
2. How would you vote if Mr. Smith was a doctor who cut off Mrs. Jones' arm to stop the spread of gangrene?
3. Dr. Smith was drunk at the time of surgery and accidentally cut off Mrs. Jones' left arm when he should have cut off her right arm. Should Dr. Smith be severely punished?

Problem #2
1. Mary is an unmarried young woman from your youth group who has gotten pregnant. Mary also helps as a substitute teacher in a class for the younger children. Should the church ask Mary to stop coming to youth events and stop teaching the younger children? What about the father - should he still be allowed at youth events?

2. How would you vote if you found out that Mary has been sleeping with three different boyfriends? (After asking for their reasons for voting the way they did, ask the participants if the congregation should be concerned about "how" Mary got pregnant—Was she raped? Was it a one-time slip-up? Is she promiscuous?)
3. The church has no business in Mary's morality. (Agree or disagree.)

Encourage discussion about the differences in each situation. Close with the following wrap-up:
- *Do rules change for given situations?*
- *Are there any rules that never change?*

2. CONNECT 10 minutes

Sometimes the rules change for different situations. What might be right in some situations might just as well be wrong in another situation.

Finding the right path in times of confusion is a "John the Baptist job"—making straight paths in the wilderness (Luke 3:3-6).

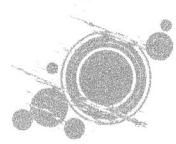

Look at the second list of modern sayings that you prepared before meeting. Point out that sayings which contradict each other can't both be right at the same time. As a group, name situations in which each of the sayings is "right." Also have the participants come up with situations in which the sayings might be "wrong."

(**Option:** Break into two teams. One team is the "Too True Team" whose job it is to find the situations in which the proverb/wise saying is true. The second team is the "Not! Lot" who read the saying and respond "Not!" by pointing out situations where the proverb/wise saying is unhelpful.)

Have participants add "wisdom sayings" they have heard from other people and have them suggest times when the saying isn't too smart. (Example: "In for a penny; in for a pound" might not be the most wise saying for an alcoholic who doesn't know when to say when.)

3. EXPLORE THE BIBLE 10 minutes

Shift to this activity by saying: *Rules themselves may not be perfect, but if we work together we can figure the "rightness" of even contradictory rules once we look at the situations.*

Break up into teams of two or three. (In smaller groups, individuals each take a chapter.) Assign a chapter from Proverbs 10 through 22 to each of the teams. (Proverbs 10, 13, 14, 15, 16, 18, 19, 20, and 21 would be particularly good for this exercise.) Ask each team to find two proverbs to present to the group; one with which they disagree *and* one with which they agree. Have each team report on the proverbs found, present the proverb in their own words, and describe the rightness and wrongness of the proverb to the rest of the group. Note these proverbs on a piece of newsprint or chalkboard.

"A parable from a fool is worthless, because he tells it at the wrong time."

Ecclesiasticus 20:20

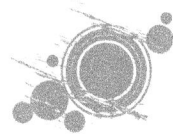

Using the third list of proverbs you prepared before the meeting, describe how some proverbs ask us to figure out right and wrong based on the situation and God's voice in our thinking. Add the following, most obviously contradictory proverbs: 26:4, "Do not answer fools according to their folly...." and 26:5, "Answer fools according to their folly ...."

Point out that biblical wisdom literature is unique in its understanding that humans can figure out right and wrong. Some Bible passages (like the Ten Commandments) are understood to be rock-solid rules for all time. Other Bible passages, like Proverbs, are invitations to learn how to figure out right from wrong. With wisdom literature, we learn to listen for God's directing in our experience and common sense. In so doing, we learn that God has the ability to speak in different situations with a different voice.

> "If one man says, 'You're a donkey,' don't mind; if two say so, be worried; if three say so, get a saddle."
>
> Adapted from Midrash: Genesis Rabbah, 45:10

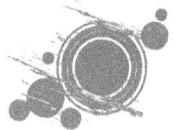

4. APPLY 10 minutes

If "truth" is impacted by experience, and if "truth" changes in different situations, what is our job as followers of Jesus when trying to make decisions? Our job is to listen as a group for the changing mystery of God's breath in each situation and name it together. When governed by the Spirit, the group, more so than the individual, can name the truth.

Sifting through the proverbs of the Bible and through the popular sayings of our own time forces us to recognize that these wise sayings need some discernment and insight before they are tossed into every situation. Just watching the way the world works is enough to inform us that rules generally don't apply to every possible situation (that's called "deontological ethics"). But this doesn't mean that we can individually just choose which ones are right and which ones are wrong for each situation (that's called "situation ethics"). Instead, we are to look at right and wrong as a community of faith and decide together what is right or wrong based on the situation and based on our understood source of truth—namely, God's voice through scripture and the Spirit.

To illustrate how a community can work with ethical situations, tell Dr. Dale Brown's story of a congregation that faced a situation similar to one in our Focus section (Problem #2). The congregation was torn between two "truths." On the one hand, the congregation had to somehow recognize that what the girl did was wrong. On the other hand, the congregation believed that she belonged with them; the young woman must be fully forgiven.

The congregation held a meeting in which they heard the woman confess her guilt. Then the congregation pronounced the young woman guilty of fornication and "removed" her from the congregation. Then, immediately after kicking her out of the congregation, they held another vote and voted her back into the congregation. All the other women in the congregation were required to give her a kiss and every man was required to shake her hand. The members of the congregation were told not to talk about the incident again. (If your participants are shrewd, they should raise the question about how the father of the child should be treated also.)

(**Note:** You might even enact the story as you tell it. Send a girl out the door, vote her back into the group, etc.)

5. RESPOND 15 minutes

The reason for the existence of proverbs is that warnings are to be shared with others. Youth often have insights about parish life that would be helpful to hear. What is more important, youth are looked up to by junior high and younger kids. When youth speak, younger kids listen!

Youth, like everyone else, unfortunately, sometimes get it wrong. We can all remember times when we got advice from a friend who meant well but who got everything messed up. The way to guard against giving rotten advice is (1) learn from your experiences, and (2) give advice that is tested by a group. Therefore:

Have participants look through the list of proverbs collected during the Explore the Bible exercise. Have teams of two or three pick a proverb that speaks to them in their situation. Have participants "translate" the proverb into their own words; have it make sense to their lives. Then publish the results of your proverb translations for yourselves **OR** for a wider audience. Choose one or more of the following:

1. Attach these new translations of ancient proverbs to the "Life is Tough Enough...So Get Smart!" poster in your meeting room.
2. Put your "Life's Tough" posters in a place where others from the parish can read them.

LOOK AHEAD

All this business about living the right kind of life, discerning right from wrong, and following the right path (even when it seems to double back in the wrong direction) is hard work. There must be a payoff, right? Right! Next time we'll look at the payoff.

For next session, gather several collections of rules (*Robert's Rules of Order*, rules of the road, school rules, etc.). Also bring nine magazines, a pointer, one large metal basin, a candle, and matches.

3. Type up the proverbs for a page in the church newsletter.
4. Make "Get Smart" bookmarks with the original translation on one side and the new translation on the other.

In each case, have the participants arrive at the best, most real proverbs by discussing and deciding together which ones are worth publishing.

INSIGHTS FROM SCRIPTURE

Wisdom literature spans a wide variety of topics. Here you can find wise sayings that direct our living in the areas of sexuality, male/female relationships, work, rest, relationships of children and parents, talking too much, talking too little, loss of one's reputation, poverty and wealth, and others.

As we read through these proverbs, an occasional problem arises. Sometimes the problem is in the fact that some proverbs contradict each other. At other times, we find that today's world can't support the authority of the proverb without some sort of disclaimer. Surprisingly, the sages of old didn't make a big deal about contradictory proverbs. It was understood that the concept of wisdom included some discernment and looked to the community of faith to support and interpret the wisdom of each saying.

In each category, and within even contradictory proverbs, the message is the same, "There is a right way and a wrong way to live." This should come as no surprise to those who read their Bibles. That's been the message from the very beginning. What is a surprise, however, is the way in which God gets the message across.

The Bible is a delightful confession of God's ability to reach out to the widest possible variety of people in a variety of ways. It is sometimes surprising to those of us who spend our spiritual lives looking for direct revelation from God, to stumble upon intricate messages of love embedded within creation. "When people want to know more about God," observes writer Barbara Brown Taylor, "the son of God tells them to pay attention to the lilies of the field and the birds of the air, to women kneading bread and workers lining up for their pay" (*An Altar in the World*). Sometimes we would do well to pay attention to the activity of God within the natural world and the reasonableness of God's creation.

In Proverbs 8:22-31 it says that Wisdom (pictured as female) was with God at creation. She was created first (before anything else) and was beside God while the world was being formed. In fact, the image is that of a child dancing alongside the Creator (see 8:30). Tony Campolo preaches in a sermon that God didn't create a field of wildflowers with one big bang, but that as God created each individual flower, a child's voice arose out of creation and said, "Do it again! Do it again!"

This is the image of Wisdom who was God's voice of childlike delight at creation, "rejoicing in the inhabited world and delighting in the human race" (8:31). The teachers of old looked for that delight-filled voice in each situation. They looked, and found God's image springing forth in untold ways when they saw the order of the world and the reasonableness of life.

The picture of Wisdom in our Bible is that she still walks beside us and watches us move through life. In those moments when we make great choices and wise decisions, she's there cheering, "Do it again! Do it again." The stirring of a group as it discerns right from wrong can be described as the Spirit of Wisdom dancing and singing, "Do it again!"

"Wisdom is God's power in action; for without it, everything is but theory."

The Mezeritzer Rabbi

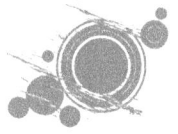

SESSION 3

IF I'M GOOD, EVERYTHING WILL TURN OUT OKAY?? »»

»» KEY VERSE

The Lord's curse is on the house of the wicked, but he blesses the abode of the righteous. (Prov. 3:33)

Paraphrase: The house of the wicked is plagued by God, but the righteous receive a home of blessing.

»» FAITH STORY

Proverbs 3

»» FAITH FOCUS

If we are honest with ourselves, believers often face the question, "Does faith work?" Wisdom literature suggests that people who follow God's path are blessed; people who do not follow God's path open themselves to be cursed. A God-directed lifestyle has a deep reward.

»» SESSION GOAL

Guide participants to recognize that trust and obedience, while not easy, have their rewards; following God's path brings a deep richness to life.

»» Materials needed and advance preparation

- Instruct one person on how to play the game Psychic Hotline (see Focus).
- Nine magazines (see Focus)
- A long pointer (broom handle, yardstick, walking stick)
- Several collections of rules (*Robert's Rules of Order*, rules of the road, school rules, etc.)
- Copies of the handout sheet for Session 3
- Bibles
- Newsprint and markers
- Metal basin, candle, hymnbooks, small slips of paper and pencils, matches (*Option A, Respond*)

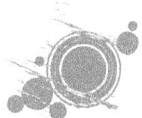

TEACHING PLAN

1. FOCUS 10 minutes

Play the game called Psychic Hotline. Lay nine magazines on the floor in a 3x3 square. Next, inform the group that you will send one person out of the room and when she or he returns, that person will be able to identify which of the nine magazines was selected during their absence.

Send the prepared person out of the room. Have the rest of the group choose one magazine. Call the person back into the room. Use the pointer to point to any of the magazines on the floor and ask, "Is it this one?" The prepared person will answer no until you point to the correct magazine at which time he or she will say yes.

Trick: (How to prepare your person.) The first time you ask, "Is this the one?" point to the spot of the magazine which corresponds to the location of the secretly selected magazine. For example, if the upper-left magazine was selected, point to the upper-left corner of any magazine when asking, "Is it this one?" If the center magazine was the one selected by the group, point to a magazine's center when asking, "Is it this one?"

Hint: You may wish to say a few "magical" words during the first pointing (e.g., "Hocus-pocus, fix and focus! Is it this one?") just to throw off the more observant people.

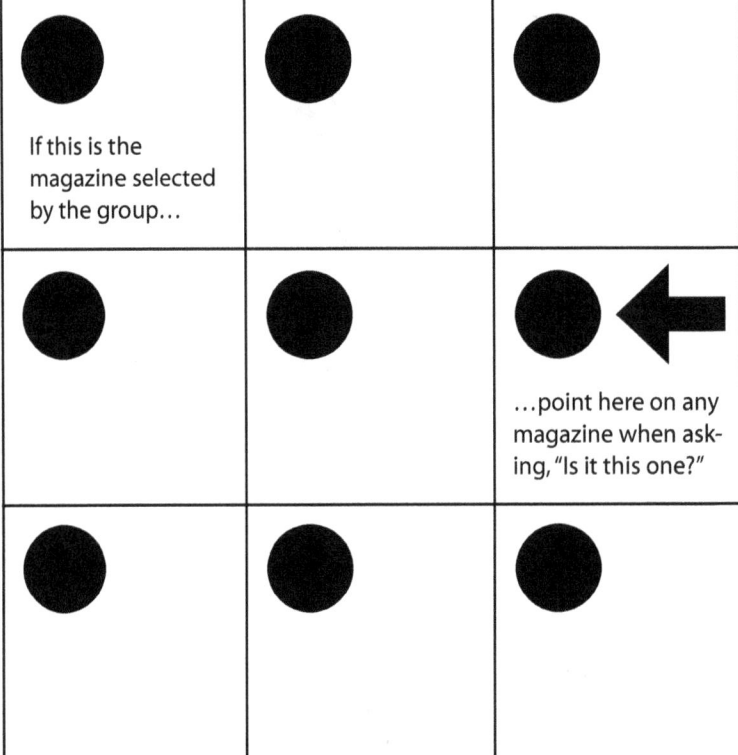

Do this several times until someone else catches on to the trick. Then send that person out of the room to see if they've really caught on. If they have, let them use the pointer while you or the prepared person go out of the room. Continue the game (making it more obvious each time) until most have caught on. Close the exercise and explain the strategy to those who don't get it.

2. CONNECT 10 minutes

Talk together about how important it was that the pointer knew the rules and followed them. In fact, if the person pointing to the magazines didn't follow the rules, no one in the group would have ever been able to pick the right magazine. Without following the rules, the game just wouldn't work.

Bring out your collection of rules and talk about each one. Ask: *In what way is each set of rules used to improve the lives of people in society?* Help participants recognize how rules help them. Even though they may not feel like stopping at a stoplight, they're surely glad that other people do, especially when they're in the middle of the intersection.

Suggest that there are good rules (just law) and there are bad rules, and some fall into both categories depending on your point of view (like registration of firearms). Have the group name rules that are good and rules that are bad. Recognize with them that it is easier to come up with good rules than bad rules because for the most part, as a society we get rid of bad rules. Emphasize that people who follow good rules generally live longer, pay fewer fines, and are less dangerous than people who do not. Good rules are good.

3. EXPLORE THE BIBLE 15 minutes

Shift to this activity by saying: *The Creator has woven rules into life so that it works—and makes life easier. Proverbs teaches us those basic life rules…*

Distribute handout sheets, assign verses to different people in the room, and give them a few moments to study their section. Then have them stand before the group and read the verse(s) aloud in their best "TV preacher" voice. Have them finish their reading (according to the instructions on the handout) with an "off-the-top-of-the-head," one-sentence sermon for their entire section. Notice that Proverbs suggests time and time again that people who follow the rules of life will live within God's good graces. Those who don't follow the rules are in for a tough life.

Point out that chapter three is divided into five sections. Ask different people to read each of the sections (1-12, 13-20, 21-26, 27-32, 33-35). Each proverb is divided into two verses. Therefore, have the participants read two verses at a time, pausing between each set of two, and then reading the next two until their whole section is done, at which point they will preach their "sermon." As each full section is finished and the "sermon" delivered, talk about the structure, the reasoning, and the relative worth of each. Some possible conversation-starters are:

- The first six doublets (1-2, 3-4, 5-6, 7-8, 9-10, 11-12) have the traditional "Do this; get that" structure. **Make a list** (verbally or on paper) of the activity ("Do this!") and its reward ("Get that!"). Can the group think of places where they've seen these proverbs come true?

- The second section (13-14, 15-16, 17-18, 19-20) is a poem about Lady Wisdom. This is the middle of the chapter; it represents the heart of the matter. Notice how many of the things we desire are produced by wisdom. **Make a list** (life, wealth, joy, etc.). A key phrase is verse 18 ("She is a tree of life to those who lay hold of her; those who hold her fast are called happy"). Like the Native American practice of sitting with your back against a big oak tree in order to renew your strength, hugging the solid tree of wisdom will renew your courage and confidence.

- The third section (21-22, 23-24, 25-26) continues the doublet pattern with instruction about how wisdom will change your life and give you more confidence. **Name together** each of the fears listed in this section (nightmares, anxiety, fear in calamities) and talk about how common those are in human experience. Then **name the strengths** promised by wisdom.

- The chapter is rounded off (27-28, 29-30, 31-32) with some prohibitions for good measure. Don't do this. Don't do that. Don't even think about the other. Take a look together at each of these prohibitions and interpret what they mean for today's youth. Note that "perversion" is used here (31-32) as it is most often in the Bible, to talk about violence, not strange sex practices.

- Verses 33-35 close the chapter with a teaching about God's relationship with the wise and God's disapproval of the wicked. Ask: *Are these proverbs talking about a God who tosses lightning bolts at naughty people? Or is it a more general comment about the way God set up the world?*

HINT

Notice that chapter 3 is divided into sayings which are all two verses long (with the exception of the last one). This "doublet" structure is a favorite of Proverbs.

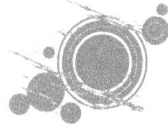

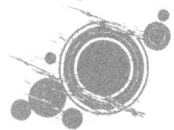

Wise people go through life praying that God will change them, and stop worrying about changing the laws of nature.

4. APPLY 7 minutes

Give a "rapid-fire law course." Have the group name natural laws—ways the world works—while you jot them on one half of a sheet of newsprint. Encourage laws like "Gravity makes things fall," "Sex makes babies," and "Ice makes your fingers numb." After you've collected a short list, write beside each law the good and the bad points about having such a law. Ice, for example, makes strained ligaments stop swelling (good) as well as causes frostbite (bad). Talk together about laws of nature.

Sometimes we think God is just a crotchety old guy who came up with a whole bunch of rules to keep people in line. We get frustrated when we think that God just made up these hundreds of rules for no good reason and that if we don't follow them, we'll go to hell.

Proverbs paints a different picture. God has created a world in which there are certain realities (like gravity). God has been good to us by providing guides to behavior (like not jumping off of tall buildings) so that we can get the most out of this life and avoid as much pain as possible.

The question is not whether the world will change for us; reality will stay the same whether we like gravity or not. The question is not whether or not the rules will change; they are directly connected with reality. The only question that remains is whether or not *we* will adjust and trust God's guidance and obey the instruction. It's really up to us. Some people go through life praying that God will change the rules. Wise people go through life praying that God will change *them*, and stop worrying about changing the laws of nature.

5. RESPOND 5 minutes

>> **Option A:** Light a candle and set it in a metal basin. If your group likes to sing, sing ""The Summons" or other similar song, **OR** read the words of the song aloud. Call each participant to name silently one part of their lives where they will turn to trust and obey God's guidance. Have the participants write on a slip of paper a word which represents this part of their lives. As a sign of faith and release, invite the participants to burn these slips of paper in the flame and allow the paper to fall into the basin.

Close with a prayer thanking God for each person in the group. Ask God to strengthen each of them so that they might follow Wisdom's warning and walk in the paths God has charted through this world.

>> **Option B:** Name heroes and heroines from the local church or the Church universal who have followed God's guidance in tough situations. These might include:

- St. Óscar Romero, bishop and defendant of the poor in El Salvador
- Blessed Franz Jägerstätter, Austrian youth executed for refusing to join Hitler's army, despite the urging of his family and his pastor
- Dorothy Day, co-founder of the Catholic Worker movement
- Faithful people who practiced peace while the nation tried to convince them to go to war
- Local people who stand out as leading God-guided lives even when faced with tempting or difficult choices

Close with a prayer thanking God for each of these saints of faith. Lift up their decisions as times in which God has spoken with a special voice to humanity. Thank God for each person in the group and ask for strength to walk along God's way.

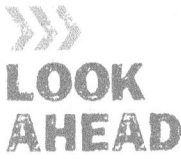

LOOK AHEAD

The idea of punishment and reward remains a problem in our thinking of God's activity in the world. Next time, we'll look at the most detailed attempt in the Bible at answering that problem: the story of Job. You'll need to get four actors for the next session.

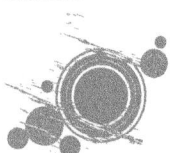

# INSIGHTS FROM SCRIPTURE

The book of Proverbs is made up of different styles of wise sayings. Some are poems consisting of several lines. Others are riddles (Proverbs 30 has several examples). Still others are *acrostics*, in which each verse of the poem starts with a new letter of the Hebrew alphabet (31:10-31). In chapter three, the proverbs are constructed as doublets—two sayings in parallel. This is by far the most frequent style.

Chapter 3 is dedicated to the rather optimistic view of reality proposed by early wisdom literature. Being good (equated with wisdom) brings life, riches, and honors (3:2, 4, and 10); foolishness (equated with wickedness) brings a divine curse, scorn, and disgrace (3:33-35). Since belief in an afterlife was not yet part of the faith tradition, rewards mentioned in these proverbs were thought of as being delivered in this world, not the next. It is a picturesque outline of reality—an idyllic understanding of reward and punishment.

The teachers of ancient wisdom were not naive, however. They were willing to acknowledge the mystery of God's activity in the world. Even those who were righteous could expect a little pain (3:11-12) in life. Yet, for the most part, good folks got good things; foolish or wicked folks did not.

There is a delicate balance carried through all of wisdom literature. In talking about the ways in which people can bring themselves good things, there is a temptation to believe that God is present in life to give us what we want. This is a vending-machine theology (put in the right money, push the right buttons, and a candy-bar comes out). It is easy to read this kind of theology into wisdom literature. There are rewards for right living. Sometimes the rewards are "from God" (3:26) and at other times, the reward is within Wisdom herself (3:16).

To balance our tendency to want God, angels, or idols to cater to our every whim, wisdom reports that the world is structured by God in such a way that right living yields better outcomes. Wisdom wants us to understand that we are here to do what God wants and in so doing we will find ourselves moving into joy and completeness.

"It is my desire to do God's will, not that God will do my will."

The Gerer Rabbi

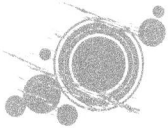

Preach it!

This is your big break—a chance to "preach" a one-sentence sermon!

In Real Life
Exploring tough questions facing youth today

Study your section according to the instructions below. When signaled, stand and read your assigned verses in your best "TV preacher" voice. Or maybe a street preacher. Finish your reading with an "off-the-top-of-the-head," one-sentence sermon for the entire section. Notice that Proverbs suggests time and time again that people who follow the laws of life will live within God's good graces. Those who don't are in for a tough life.

Notice how Proverbs chapter three is divided into five sections. Different people will read each of the sections (1-12, 13-20, 21-26, 27-32, 33-35). Each proverb is divided into two verses. Therefore, read two verses at a time, pausing between each set of two. Read the next two until your whole section is done, then preach your one-sentence "sermon" summing it up.

- **Section 1:** The first six doublets (1-2, 3-4, 5-6, 7-8, 9-10, 11-12) have the traditional "Do this; get that" structure. **Make a list** (verbally or on paper) of the activity ("Do this!") and its reward ("Get that!"). Can you think of places where you've seen these proverbs come true?
- **Section 2:** (13-14, 15-16, 17-18, 19-20) is a poem about Lady Wisdom. This is the middle of the chapter; it represents the heart of the matter. Notice how many of the things we desire are produced by wisdom. **Make a list** (life, wealth, joy, etc.). A key phrase is verse 18 ("She is a tree of life to those who lay hold of her; those who hold her fast are called happy"). Like the Native American practice of sitting with your back against a big oak tree in order to renew your strength, hugging the solid tree of wisdom will renew your courage and confidence.
- **Section 3:** (21-22, 23-24, 25-26) continues the doublet pattern with instruction about how wisdom will change your life and give you more confidence. **Name together** each of the fears listed in this section (nightmares, anxiety, fear in calamities) and talk about how common those are in human experience. Then **name the strengths** promised by wisdom.
- **Section 4:** (27-28, 29-30, 31-32) rounds off the chapter with some prohibitions for good measure. Don't do this. Don't do that. Don't even think about the other. Take a look together at each of these prohibitions and interpret what they mean for today. Note that "perversion" is used here (31-32) as it is most often in the Bible, to talk about violence, not strange sex practices.
- **Section 5:** Verses 33-35 close the chapter with a teaching about God's relationship with the wise and God's disapproval of the wicked. Ask yourself, *Are these proverbs talking about a God who tosses lightning bolts at naughty people? Or is it a more general comment about the way God set up the world?*

HINT

Notice that chapter 3 is divided into sayings which are all two verses long (with the exception of the last one). This "doublet" structure is a favorite of Proverbs.

Permission is granted to photocopy this handout for use with this session.

SESSION 4

WHY DO BAD THINGS HAPPEN TO GOOD PEOPLE? >>>

>>> KEY VERSES

[Job said,] "Shall we receive the good at the hand of God, and not receive the bad?" (Job 2:10b)
Paraphrase: Do we get the blessings from God and refuse the rough spots?
    and
Then the Lord answered Job out of the whirlwind: "Who is this that darkens counsel by words without knowledge?" (Job 38:1-2)
Paraphrase: After this God answered Job from within the whirlwind: "Is this an advanced degree in ignorance that counsels without knowing?"

>>> FAITH STORY

Job 1–7, and 38

>>> FAITH FOCUS

A direct challenge to the heart of early wisdom is the story of Job, a totally righteous man who suffered unjustly. Unjust suffering is a frequent complaint of adolescents. Why does God allow suffering? What do we do when people are in pain? When we look at the suffering of innocent people in our world, we begin to challenge our assumption about God. What is discovered in Job's story, however, is that it is from *within* our suffering that God becomes more clearly understood. Perhaps it is enough to know that God speaks to us from inside our suffering.

>>> SESSION GOAL

Guide youth, crowded by strong notions of what's fair, to open themselves to the idea that God speaks from inside suffering.

>>> Materials needed and advance preparation

- Select four people to play the parts listed in Focus, and give them their parts to study (on the handout sheet for this session).
- Bibles
- Paper and pencils/pens
- Alert other Sunday school classes that you'll be interrupting them with a commercial message from Job (*Option A, Respond*).

YOUTH AND JUSTICE

Adolescence is a time of emotional and spiritual development when there is a strong focus on justice. Youth can report quickly about things that aren't fair in school, at home, and in the world at large. It's a genetic or hormonal gift of being young!

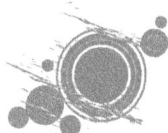

"Love, in reason's terms, answers nothing… conquers nothing– certainly not death–certainly not chance. What love does is to affirm. It affirms the worth of life in spite of life. It affirms the wonder and the beauty of the human creature, mortal and insignificant and ignorant though he be…"

Archibald MacLeish, *J.B.: A Play in Verse* based on the story of Job

TEACHING PLAN

1. FOCUS 20 minutes

Dramatize "Visit the Dying Pillar."

Call on the four actors who prepared the play (descriptions are on the handout sheet for this session) and invite the audience to watch and listen closely. The actors should work into their improvised scripts the information about each character's situation and attitude.

You as leader can set the stage by saying something like:

> The scene is a hospital room. In the bed, debilitated by a rare disease, is **Pat Donley**, well-respected pillar of the faith community. When people have had questions about God, Pat has had the answers and has been a spiritual resource for others. Until this moment, Pat was feeling closer to God than ever. If a "spiritual checkup" was given, Pat would have passed with flying colors. Now, here comes **Deacon Barry Wine** to visit… (cue the action).

Alternative: If your group is very small (or shy) consider importing adult actors from your congregation. Have these "professional" actors put on the play and do the readings in Explore.

2. CONNECT 5 minutes

When the play ends, ask the person who took the role of Pat to talk about the visitors. Ask the visitors to talk about how they felt in their roles. What did the audience see in the action? What felt right about what each visitor was doing? What felt wrong?

Talk together about how conversations with sick people change when we assume that *they deserve what they're getting*. Do we sometimes place blame on people who are innocent in their suffering? Do we ourselves sometimes feel guilty even when our sickness, loss, or error was out of our control?

On the other hand, are there times when making the suffering person feel better is just not enough? Are there times when we *do* deserve what we get? Are people who smoke just asking for lung cancer? Are we allowed to scold people who get into auto accidents when driving drunk?

Then again, what is it like to suffer *because* we have done what is right? Do we know of stories of people who suffered because they did what was right? (Examples include: Anne Frank, Jesus, Martin Luther King Jr., Oscar Romero.) Are there times when youth suffer because they stand up for what is right?

3. EXPLORE THE BIBLE 10 minutes.

Shift to this activity by saying: These questions about suffering get asked by every generation. The story of Job was written to try to answer them. Let's take a look….

Introduce the story:

> Job, a man who is absolutely innocent, finds himself suffering. While suffering, Job is visited by friends who believe that hardships come as the direct result of sin; people get what they deserve. But what does God say? (See 42:7.)

Assign three participants to take the parts of Job, Satan, and God. Have four others take the parts of the messengers, the wife, and the narrator.

Option for smaller groups: You as leader take the part of narrator, have one youth read the part of the messengers and wife, and another each for Job, Satan, and God. Together, read dramatically the story of Job as it is found in Job 1:6–2:13.

In a short talk, tell what happens in the rest of the story. Highlight the attitude of the "friends" of Job, his wife's suggestion (2:9), and Job's requests throughout (see Insights from Scripture, below). Conclude by telling how God responds to Job (from chapter 38).

4. APPLY 15 minutes

As a group, write three television commercials using the story of Job. What three points would you make, as a group, about the story? What is God trying to tell humanity in this story? Some suggestions to start you thinking are:
1. Life is not always fair.
2. Believers must learn to take the bad with the good.
3. God's voice can be heard in the middle of the stormy parts of life.

Break into groups of three with each group designing their own commercial. A commercial lasts for only 30 seconds (60 seconds at the most), so set that limit as groups present their commercials. Remember to have each commercial end with a tag line: "This message brought to you by the National Pot-sherd and Ashes League." If the group has fewer than five people, work together to create one commercial.

5. RESPOND 10 minutes

Option A: Take your commercials on the road. If you meet on Sunday morning, have your group visit other classes to "interrupt their regularly scheduled program for a special message." Groups could even suggest that interested persons contact the youth or the pastor for more information about innocent suffering and the will of God. Another tie-in would be to offer published copies of "Youth Proverbs" (the ones you've been collecting) for a small donation.

Option B: Go the extra mile. Consider sponsoring a youth mass with Job as its theme. Ask the pastor and/or liturgy committee for permission to do this. You might consider having one of the youth share a reflection after the homily, or use a bulletin insert to share the youth wisdom sayings you have been creating. Job appears on the Sunday lectionary only twice: the 5th and 12th Sundays in Ordinary Time in Year B. If it proves too difficult to time your sessions to the liturgical calendar, you might ask for special permission to change the first reading.

Instead of reading from Job, you could develop a skit based on the first three chapters of the book of Job. Perhaps you could interrupt your service with your commercial messages. Write a reflection based on the themes of each of the commercials and tie the story to the feelings of others in the parish who may also be suffering. Present the "hope" of the Job story (not just the pain) by reminding the parish that God becomes present to Job from within the whirlwind, from within his suffering.

> "When the tempest passes, the wicked are no more, but the righteous are established forever."

Proverbs 10:25

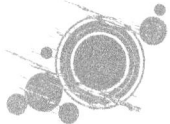

> "Wisdom, like gold ore, is mixed with stones and dust."

Moses Ibn Ezra, Shirat Yisrael

LOOK AHEAD

If you are using the extender session, next week would be a good time to do that. It continues to wrestle with the idea of innocent suffering, or suffering in the right, by looking at the wisdom tradition in the New Testament, and how the simple use wisdom.

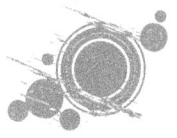

> "We are, and that is all our answer. We are and what we are can suffer. But...what suffers, loves.
> And love will live its suffering again, endure the loss of everything again and yet again and yet again in doubt, in dread, in ignorance, unanswered, over and over, with the dark before, the dark behind it... and still live... still love."
>
> Archibald MacLeish, *J.B.: A Play in Verse* based on the story of Job

> "You make the winds your messengers, fire and flame your ministers."
>
> Psalm 104:4

INSIGHTS FROM SCRIPTURE

There's no doubt about it; Job got a raw deal. He spent his life trying to do good and be good, and because of this, he suffered great hardship and personal pain. In fact, the way the story reads, if Job had been a rotten guy he may have had a better life. We are told flat out, at the beginning of the story, that the reason for Job's suffering is *because* he is absolutely blameless (1:1, 8-12). Job's trouble began when God and Satan noticed his goodness. Satan then took it as a personal challenge to toss trouble at Job in order to make him give up his goodness.

We're not talking about a little trouble; the trouble is huge. Family, servants, crops, and cattle are all lost to the horror of Satan's activity (1:13-21). And still, Job's response was to recognize God's power over all of life (1:22). This confession is basic to wisdom, which recognizes that the fear (reverence) of the Lord is the beginning of understanding (see Prov. 1:7, 29; 2:5; 8:13; 9:10; 10:27; 14:26-27; 15:16, 33; 16:6; 19:23; 23:17).

Not only is Job good for no apparent reason, he is good even after disaster comes knocking at his door. So Satan (literally: "the advocate") redoubles his efforts and gets permission from God to inflict "loathsome sores on Job from the sole of his foot to the crown of his head" (2:7). At this point even Job's wife can't understand why in the world Job would still believe in God's goodness. "Curse God, and die," she says. But still, Job responds in faith. This is exactly the opposite of what traditional wisdom literature would have us believe. In fact, his friends tell him so. When Job's three friends (Eliphaz the Temanite, Bildad the Shuhite, and Zophar the Naamathite) heard of all these troubles, "they met together to go and console and comfort him" (2:11). Their chief message was, "You must have done something to deserve this; confess your sin and things will be put right."

It's not that his friends are cold or uncaring. In fact, they wept with him, tore their robes and threw dust in the air upon their heads (signs of grief). The narrator makes a special effort to show these friends caring for Job. They even sit in the dirt with him for seven days without saying a word (2:13). Many of us wish we had friends who knew how badly we were hurting and were willing to sit with us in our pain.

Through most of the book, Job complains about the injustice of his pain. Job asks that his wrongs be brought out into the open and weighed on the scale beside his pain (Job 6:2). They are not balanced! Job's suffering is "heavier than the sand of the sea," while his life shows nothing to deserve this (1:1). So Job complains about his pain, "For the arrows of the Almighty are in me; my spirit drinks their poison; the terrors of God are arrayed against me" (Job 6:4). Like most humans, Job wants to bring God to trial and have God answer for the suffering.

After each complaint, one of Job's friends takes a turn at defending God. It is so like us to try to step in and defend God from the complaints of others. It's as though we see God as needing our help.

Each friend offers the same defense of God: "You must have done something to deserve this." As 4:8 puts it, "As I have seen, those who plow iniquity and sow trouble reap the same." They care about Job and don't want to see him prolong his suffering by refusing to confess his sin. Again, like most humans, they try to help him find *some reason* for the suffering.

Even with all this caring, however, God is not pleased with the responses of the friends (see 42:7). The old "vending-machine God" (put good things in to get good things out; put bad things in to get bad things out) was too limited and limiting an understanding of the Creator. This is a good warning to people who would dictate how God must act.

God answers Job's complaint by saying, "Where were you when I built creation?" While Job complains, "You lift me up on the wind, you make me ride on it, and you toss me about in the roar of the storm" (30:22), it is from the middle of the whirlwind, literally and figuratively, that God answers this sack-clothed, ash-covered questioner (38:1 and 40:6). The whirlwind is somewhat less frightening if we understand that God can be found at its center. In fact, the most powerful conversations we have with God come in the middle of the whirlwind—in the middle of life's trouble.

Both Nahum the prophet and the psalmist preach that "God's way is in whirlwind and storm," and that God "rides the wings of the wind." As believers, we confess that the destructive force of the storm is not the end of the story but instead a new beginning. It is invitation to understand ourselves and our Creator in a new way.

Visit the Dying Pillar

Pat Donley (respected pillar of the faith community): Pat knows more about the Bible than anyone else in the church. When people have questions about God, Pat has the answers. Pat has been a spiritual resource for other people. Until this moment, Pat was feeling closer to God than ever.

Recently, life has turned bad. Pat's whole family has been killed by a rare disease and Pat is in the hospital receiving treatment. The family home burned, most people don't come around anymore, and Pat's company is downsizing and fired Pat last week. Everything that can go wrong has gone wrong. This is a disaster of biblical proportion.

As a child, Pat learned in Sunday school that God punishes evil and rewards good. God has always been described as just and fair. God has also been described as always good, all-powerful, and all-knowing. But looking at the recent pain, death, and rash of destruction, Pat is having some trouble believing those childhood lessons. Pat has done nothing wrong to deserve this.
"Why is God doing this to me?" is Pat's anguished cry.

Deacon Barry Wine (Pat's first visitor): Barry is deeply concerned for Pat's soul. Feeling that this kind of disaster could only come to people who are being punished by God, your job as Deacon Wine is to bring Pat to a point of confession. Once there is confession, there can be salvation. Deacon Wine feels personally responsible for saving Pat's soul since Pat has obviously slipped into sin (although Deacon Wine doesn't know what kind of sin). Spend some time trying to make Pat confess.
"Repent! The end is near," is Deacon Wine's feeling.

Pastor Byran Frimstone (Gentle Shepherd): Pastor Frimstone is pretty sure that God doesn't have anything to do with sick people. Instead, Byran simply wants to make Pat feel better. The pastor would tell Pat anything to make the pain go away. Byran gets uncomfortable whenever Pat asks about the pain and trouble which have come about in life. Byran would rather Pat just stop talking about the pain and look for the good things in life. Pastor Byran is often heard saying, "We'll keep a good thought."
"Don't worry. Be happy," is Pastor Frimstone's feeling.

Angel Gabriella/Gabriel (Sent by God to check in on Pat): Gabe is a listening angel. S/he is really wanting Pat to speak about what's going on in life and to share even the most heartfelt concerns. God has been getting a whole lot of prayers for—and from—Pat. God wants Gabe to check things out. Listen to Pat and find out three things: What does Pat want to know from God; what does Pat think is happening; what is Pat telling friends about being one of God's children? Gabe's main job is to listen.
"What's up?" is Gabe's question.

Permission is granted to photocopy this handout for use with this session.

SESSION 5

LIFE'S NOT FAIR, SO WHY BOTHER? »»

KEY VERSES

There is a vanity that takes place on earth, that there are righteous people who are treated according to the conduct of the wicked, and there are wicked people who are treated according to the conduct of the righteous. I said that this also is vanity. So I commend enjoyment, for there is nothing better for people under the sun than to eat, and drink, and enjoy themselves, for this will go with them in their toil through the days of life that God gives them under the sun. (Ecclesiastes 8:14-15)

FAITH STORY

Ecclesiastes 3:1-13; 8:10-15; 9:7-10; 12:1-7

FAITH FOCUS

When we spend all our efforts trying to figure out how the world works, whether life is just or unjust, we often miss the life within the moment. Ecclesiastes, after searching for the meaning of life, draws the conclusion that God will be in charge of the way the world works; we are charged of our joy. The joy of life comes from living out the fullness of each moment as it unfolds at God's directing. This is not the same as living *for* the moment. Instead, we live fully *within* the moment but for the Creator.

SESSION GOAL

Guide participants to learn the difference between living *for* the moment and living *in* God's moment.

Materials needed and advance preparation

- Instruction cards for Third Degree game (see Focus)
- Bibles
- Chalkboard/chalk or newsprint/markers
- Copies of the handout sheet for Session 5
- A sheet of paper, envelope, and stamp for each person
- Pens or pencils

TEACHING PLAN

1./2. FOCUS/CONNECT 20 minutes

Play the game **Third Degree.** Form two teams—one composed of **inspectors** from Scotland Yard, the other of **spies**. Give each spy a card bearing one of the instructions listed below; each spy receives a different instruction. The Scotland Yard detectives then take turns asking specific spies questions, calling out the name of each spy before asking the question. Scotland Yard's goal is to eliminate all the spies by guessing their instructions. A Scotland Yard inspector may ask as many questions of as many or few spies as they choose, and may ask any question, except about the instructions the spies were given.

LIVING WITHIN THE MOMENT

When we spend all our efforts trying to figure out how the world works, whether life is just or unjust, we often miss the life within the moment. Ecclesiastes, after searching for the meaning of life, draws the conclusion that God will be in charge of the way the world works; we are charged of our joy. The joy of life comes from living out the fullness of each moment as it unfolds at God's directing. This is not the same as living *for* the moment. Instead, we live fully *within* the moment but for the Creator.

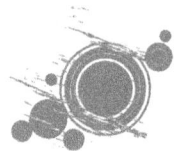

A Scotland Yard inspector may guess a spy's instructions at any time, whether or not it is his/her turn to ask a question. Each spy must answer each question always in the manner described on the card. Elimination of a spy occurs when:
- a spy gives an answer without following instructions, **OR**
- the spy's instructions are guessed correctly by Scotland Yard.

The questions continue until all the spies' instructions are guessed correctly.

Spy Instructions:
1. Lie during every answer.
2. Answer each question as though you were (name of adult leader).
3. Try to start an argument with each answer you give.
4. Always state the name of some color in your answer.
5. Always use a number in your answer.
6. Be evasive—never actually answer a question.
7. Always answer a question with a question.
8. Always exaggerate your answer.
9. Always pretend to misunderstand the question by your answer.
10. Always scratch during your answer.

Give points to the spy for each question asked prior to the instructions being guessed. For Scotland Yard, three points are scored for each correct guess of the spy's instructions.

(**Note:** For smaller groups, rotate one person as the spy and allow the remaining people to act as Scotland Yard inspectors.)

3. EXPLORE THE BIBLE 15 minutes

Shift to this activity with this mini-lecture: *Searching for a hidden instruction set requires patience and thought. Sooner or later, a pattern begins to emerge. Understanding this helps us to look more deeply for patterns in other areas of our lives.*

This is what wisdom literature is all about—looking for the patterns in life. In looking for the master instruction set, the DNA of the good life, the people who wrote wisdom sayings tried to draw a clear picture from within a confusing world.

For the most part, wisdom literature suggests that if you do good, you get goodness; if you do bad things, you get badness. It's a rather simple understanding about the way the world works. In many instances these assumptions are correct. Sometimes, however, the instructions of life seem to miss something. Think about the story of Job—sometimes good things happen to bad people and bad things happen to good people. The book of Job suggests that life isn't as simple as the vending machine system proposed by the earliest books of wisdom.

So now what? That's the question posed by the author of Ecclesiastes.

Ask three people to read the following passages aloud: **Ecclesiastes 8:10-15; 9:7-10; 12:1-7.** Remind them that Psalms, Proverbs, and Ecclesiastes are right in the middle of the Bible. Introduce the readings with some short words about the book (see Insights from Scripture section below).

Before they begin reading, write on the chalkboard or newsprint the words **Complaint**, **Proof**, **Solution**, leaving room under each for more writing. Ask the group to keep their ears open for each of these elements in the complaint of the Preacher.

After each section is read, write down the Complaint, Proof, and Solution as they are given by the group. Work together to put them into modern language rather than simply quoting from scripture.

(*Hint:* In general the complaint will read, "Life does not always reward good behavior and punish bad"; the proof will read, "Bad people get the same treatment as good people" (in the first section this reads, "Bad people are buried alongside good people when they die"); and the solution follows, "Eat, drink, and be happy within the fear of the Lord.")

Reading closely, one recognizes that this is more than just a jaded Preacher. He's got a point. He's not saying that it doesn't matter how one lives. Instead, his emphasis is on the fact that it doesn't pay to live only for the future respect of others. In the end, the good and the bad are buried side by side.

Instead, says the Preacher, live each moment to its fullest intended purpose. Eat, drink, and find joy. He is not suggesting that there is nothing more in life than the enjoyment of the moment, but that the joy within the moment is part of the living that God intends for us. Experience life *in* the now—not *for* the now.

Seen on a T-shirt: "Exercise, eat right, don't smoke, die anyway."

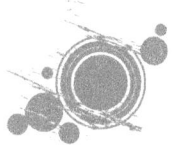

4. APPLY 5 minutes

Distribute handout sheets and read the poem there. Ask the group to think about ways in which they are like the young man in the poem. Where are the places in their lives where they are so looking forward that they cannot appreciate the present?

Add Ecclesiastes' thought for the day—eat, drink, and enjoy life—to the Youth Proverbs poster. Talk about the difference between living *in* the day *for* God's Way and living only *for* the day.

5. RESPOND 10 minutes

Make a list of "things in my life worth living for." Put this list on newsprint for everyone to see and discuss. (*Hint:* If someone names something others feel isn't worth listing, help the group see value in everyone's input. Help reword poor choices.) Talk about how Ecclesiastes would urge us to make the most out of each of these items and come up with more. Recognize together how each of these things might point to the realm of God so that our living might be *in* the moment and toward the life of God.

Have each person write a letter to themselves. In the letter have them urge themselves to make the most of their lives and to fully enjoy the gifts in their lives. Have them lift out one specific point worth celebrating in their lives and urge themselves to do something about it.

Date and sign the letters, and inform the group that you will mail the letters later as reminders to live life fully for the life God intends. (Have the group self-address envelopes before handing them in.)

Close with prayer, thanking God for each person in the group and asking God to make their joy complete.

(*Hint:* Mark your calendar now to mail the letters in about six months. Consider copying the proverb list from the newsprint and enclosing a copy with each person's letter.)

> "'And if not now, when?' asked Hillel. 'When will the now be?' The now that is now, this moment, never existed before—from the time the world was created; and this moment will never exist again. Formerly there was another now, and later there will be another now, and every now has its own special import and function."
>
> Hasidic saying

 # INSIGHTS FROM SCRIPTURE

Ecclesiastes, or Qoheleth (as the Hebrew has it), is either the title or name of the individual writing this book. If it is a title, we would probably translate it, "Assemblyman" or "Preacher." If the book is named after a person, the proper name would be "Qoheleth." The RSV and KJV translate this word "Preacher" (NIV: "Teacher," NEB: "Speaker"), while the New Jerusalem Bible uses "Qoheleth" as a proper name. Whoever he is—teacher, preacher, or speaker—we see here the honest lament of an educated middle-aged (or older) man searching for meaning in life.

"'Meaningless! Meaningless!' says the Teacher. 'Utterly meaningless! Everything is meaningless'" (1:2 NIV). The RSV and KJV word "vanity" does not adequately translate the feeling in this passage. The author is suggesting something empty (NEB), futile (JB), utterly insubstantial and insignificant. "I applied my mind to...wisdom," (1:13) says the preacher. "My mind has had great experience in...knowledge" (1:16). But even with great quantities of knowledge and wisdom he realizes that this is a "chasing after wind" (1:17). It is as impossible to capture meaning as it is to capture the wind. In fact, the search for meaning has led to even greater suffering (1:18).

Qoheleth understood that the immature faith he had been taught could make him "good" (as one would refer to a child who follows instructions) but could not make him whole. Finally Qoheleth suggests that we "eat, drink, and find happiness." Yet he is not giving in to an answer of easy hedonism after searching all his life for ultimate meaning. He is shifting gears.

In his book *When All You Ever Wanted Isn't Enough*, Rabbi Harold Kushner interprets Qoheleth's refrain as, "If logic tells us that life is a meaningless accident...don't give up on life. Give up on logic. If logic tells you that in the long run, nothing makes a difference because we all die and disappear, then *don't live in the long run*. Learn to savor the moment."

This may be related to the concept of joy in the New Testament. Joy is made complete by the timing and presence of the Messiah. "I have said these things to you so that my joy may be in you, and that your joy may be complete" (John 15:11 NRSV). Eat, drink, and find joy!

Present Tense
by Jason Lehman
(written when he was 14)

In Real Life

Exploring tough questions facing youth today

It was Spring.
But it was Summer I wanted,
The warm days,
And the great outdoors.

It was Summer.
But it was Fall I wanted,
The colorful leaves,
And the cool, dry air.

It was Fall.
But it was Winter I wanted,
The beautiful snow,
And the joy of the holiday season.

It was Winter.
But it was Spring I wanted,
The warmth,
And the blossoming of nature.

I was a child.
But it was adulthood I wanted,
The freedom,
And the respect.

I was twenty.
But it was thirty I wanted,
To be mature,
And sophisticated.

I was middle-aged.
But it was twenty I wanted,
The youth,
And the free spirit.

I was retired.
But it was middle-age I wanted,
The presence of mind,
Without limitations.

My life was over.

But I never got what I wanted.

»» LIVING WITHIN THE MOMENT

When we spend all our efforts trying to figure out how the world works, whether life is just or unjust, we often miss the life within the moment. God will be in charge of the way the world works; we are charged for our joy. The joy of life comes from not from living for the moment, but living fully *within* the moment and for the Creator.

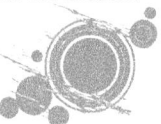

Permission is granted to photocopy this handout for use with this session.

>>> **EXTENDER SESSION**
(best used after Session 4)

MORE ON PROVERBS

>>> **Option A:** Proverbs Are Like a Box of Chocolates

>>> **SESSION GOAL**

Along with the basic understanding that proverbs are a good teaching tool for persons of all levels of intelligence, help participants begin creating a bank of proverbs to use when faced with adversity.

>>> **SESSION PLAN**

Together view the movie *Forrest Gump* with an eye out for proverbs. Prior to the beginning of the movie, instruct participants to listen for proverbs. Remind them what a proverb is and how they might sound. Give them cues to watch for: "My mother always told me...." Just as important, however, ask participants to be aware of where and why the proverbs are being used.

During the movie, have participants catch all the "proverbs" uttered by Forrest and others, and call them out as you jot them on a piece of newsprint while the movie is running. Put a star beside those uttered by Forrest when he finds himself in particularly difficult (or embarrassing) situations.

Talk together after the movie is over about how proverbs were used for Forrest. Point out the use of proverbs to:

a. give structure to life,
b. guard against negative impact from the world, and
c. give direction in times of choice.

Remind each other that biblical proverbs also point in these directions.

>>> **Materials needed and advance preparation**

- Show the movie *Forrest Gump* (Option A)
- Media player
- Newsprint and markers
- Show a "Jesus" film that includes the Sermon on the Mount (Option B)

>> **Option B:** Hearing the Proverbs of Christ

Review the Sermon on the Mount (Matthew 5, especially 1-16).

>> SESSION GOAL

Encourage participants to see Jesus' radical Sermon on the Mount as a guide for living, not just an abstract understanding of life somewhere else.

>> SESSION PLAN

Together, read through (or watch) the Sermon on the Mount. Several of a variety of "Jesus" films are good for this exercise. Play the portions focusing on the Sermon on the Mount, and jot down the proverbs found there (the beatitudes are a good place to start). Discuss how different religious traditions interpret the beatitudes. Some see these as wonderful goals for a future world. Others view them as mandates for living as saints. Still others argue that these are signposts to spiritual maturity in all believers.

We might best see them as proverbs of the new life in God. These are Jesus' promises about how the new realm works. Looking at the list of the proverbs Jesus utters, note how they are similar or different from the type of sayings in the book of Proverbs. You might even find rewards in arguing whether they are "true" or not.

In Real Life
Exploring tough questions facing youth today

CLUELESS AND CALLED
Discipleship and the Gospel of Mark

What does it take to be a disciple? This study of the Gospel of Mark focuses on the requirements for following Jesus' way and the abundant life that is ours as a result. (5 sessions)

DO MIRACLES HAPPEN?
Signs and Wonders in the Gospel of John

The greatest miracle, recorded in John 1:14 and 3:16, is the miracle of God's love that became flesh and lived among us. But John also included examples of what we more traditionally think of as miracles: the wonder of abundance from little; healing; signs of impossibility and faith; and the resurrection. (5 sessions)

DO THE RIGHT THING
Ethics Shaped by Faith

How do you know what's right and what's wrong? Even when you figure it out, the right thing is often the unpopular or unpleasant choice. This unit offers participants a clearer sense of what it means to claim a faith identity, a foundation that can help them sort out the gritty details of ethics shaped by faith.
(6 sessions)

FIGHT RIGHT
A Christian Approach to Conflict Resolution

This unit will help youth understand conflict and its function. They will learn how they can be honest and loving, and explore how conflict can be used for positive results. They will also learn ways to enhance their communication skills. 1 Corinthians. (5 sessions)

GOD IS A WARRIOR?
Violence in the Bible

The Bible challenges us to be reconciled to one another and work for justice. So what do we do with the stories that seem to condone violence or even encourage it? A discussion of issues in the Old and New Testaments. (6 sessions)

HOW DO YOU KNOW?
Wisdom in the Bible

Wisdom literature teaches us that we gain knowledge of the world, ourselves, and God through experience and observation. This unit provides practical, hands-on wisdom to help young people avoid life's snares and grow closer to God. Proverbs, Job, Ecclesiastes. (5 sessions)

HOW TO BE A TRUE FRIEND
The Bible Reveals Friendship's Heart

To be a friend takes skill. Help youth discover the secrets of friendship through various stories from the Old and New Testament. (6 sessions)

HOW TO READ THE BIBLE
Building Skills for Bible Study

What kind of book is the Bible? What does this book mean to me? This unit looks at the Bible as revelation, as history, as literature. Selected scripture. (5 sessions)

KEEPING THE GARDEN
A Faith Response to God's Creation

If Christians believe that God made the world, we do not need any more compelling reason to care for it than that God has handed us a treasure to hold and protect. This unit gets beyond trendy environmentalism and challenges youth to see environmental awareness as a religious issue. Genesis. (6 sessions)

MANTRAS, MENORAHS, AND MINARETS
Encountering Other Faiths

How is Christianity different from other faiths? Why do others believe the way they do? This study can give youth a new appreciation for the uniqueness of Jesus. Selected scripture. (5 sessions)

SALT, LIGHT, AND THE GOOD LIFE
The Beatitudes and the Sermon on the Mount

What can youth expect in a life of discipleship? This unit explores the Sermon on the Mount under four main sections: the Beatitudes, Salt and Light, Jesus and the Law, and Heavenly Teachings. Matthew 5. (6 sessions)

A SPECK IN THE UNIVERSE
The Bible on Self-Esteem and Peer Pressure

Discover God's unconditional love and acceptance of all people. This study will show positive ways to have one's life make a difference, and help youth find ways to resist negative peer pressure and turn it into positive action. (6 sessions)

THE RADICAL REIGN
Parables of Jesus

Jesus used parables to reveal what the kingdom of God is like, and how God relates to us. This study highlights how the parables reveal God's reign as radically different from the world we live in, and what that means for the Christian life. (6 sessions)

TESTING THE WATERS
Basic Tenets of Faith

Discover the biblical roots for the central Christian concepts of covenant, community, and baptism. This short course is a way to test the (baptismal) waters of Christianity before diving in, or review the basics for those who already have. (6 sessions)

WHO IS GOD?
Engaging the Mystery

God is beyond human comprehension, yet desires to be known. These sessions focus on the way we get clues about and glimpses of God from the Bible, God's creation, and church tradition. Selected scripture. (5 sessions)